THE BOOK OF TRIADS

THE BOOK OF TRIADS
J. A. Gucci

First Edition

ISBN: 978-1-972788-02-8

Printed in the United States of America

TABLE OF CONTENTS

PREFACE

This book is composed entirely of triads.

Each poem is structured as three stanzas. Each
stanza, three lines. Each line corresponds to a
layer of perception:
matter, mind, and being.

There are no metaphors here.
What appears symbolic is not. What seems
obscure is exact.
You may not always recognize what you're
seeing —
but the pressure behind each line is real.

The system of triads is not meant to be
decoded.
It is meant to be followed.

Interpretation is not the author's burden.
Connection is not enforced.
The reader is responsible for their own
compression.

This is a book about how meaning folds.
About how pressure becomes pattern.
About the trace left when perception moves
through form.

Each triad is a fold.
Each fold is a pressure system.
Each pressure system is a map.

Follow nothing.
Read closely.

— J. A. Gucci

FOREWORD

by Dr. Lang Reuden, Cartologist Emeritus
Institute of Pattern Theory (Retired)

I've seen texts attempt to disguise systems as
poetry.

This one does the opposite.

The Book of Triads is not a book of poems. It's a
pressure map. Each unit is a fold; each fold
holds a tension you don't notice until it
changes you. The lines don't invite
interpretation — they resist it. The system
doesn't ask for faith — it functions.

J. A. Gucci has built a language that doesn't
care what you think. That's what makes it
honest. This is not abstraction. It is
compression.

Most readers will read this once and move on.
A few will return, slowly.
One or two will start to see the trace.

That will be enough.
This book doesn't teach.
It leaves evidence.

— *Lang Reuden*
Berlin / Los Angeles
April 2026

AUTHOR'S NOTE

This book was not written for clarity.
It was written for pressure.

Each triad began as a point of contact — an
image, a force, a fold. The system emerged
slowly. I followed it. I refined it. I didn't invent
it.

No metaphor was used in the making of these
pages. The reader will find none provided —
but many implied. That's their burden.

Each poem stands alone.
Together, they trace a system:
a cartology of compression.
Mind, matter, being — three lines per stanza.
Three stanzas per triad.
Three arcs: ground, field, echo.

This book rewards rereading, not explanation.
Some poems were removed.
Some folded inward.

Some survived the pressure.
What remains is the record.

— J. A. Gucci

SECTION I — GROUND

I. THE TRIAD OF WILL

Shuddering lintel.
Free-fall in a spaghetti field.
Sea stump.

Gale pummels a caprock.
Eggy asphalt absorbing light.
Alluvial fan.

Warm air falling upward.
Kiting hawk alula.
Lizard footprints on water.

II. THE TRIAD OF PRESSURE

Chassis cooking on a chaussee.
Shivering hand.
Whale tail—oil on water.

Heat haze—a cold diamond.
Memory twitching on a nerve.
Static radio hiss.

Rocks in a crotch bouncing.
Windy Yardang fields.
A smile, a squint—gullies.

III. THE TRIAD OF TENSION

Steamer collides with graupel.
Fluttering on a wet web.
A crack—snow plumes.

Sealed soda can.
Running faucet—plugged tub.
Sweat.

Hissing valve.
Pleated sheets in a cleft.
Crusty lead terminals.

SECTION II — FIELD

IV. THE TRIAD OF DISTORTION

Severed sound wave.
Dark quoin on bright sky.
Cheetah spots.

Mie scattering.
Rain.
Alpenglow.

Air sucked into smoke.
Muffled bugle in downwind.
Haze.

V. THE TRIAD OF SIGNAL

Krill claw snap.
Whistling Karren.
Singing sand dune.

Sooty Owl whoos.
Silent rumble in my sole.
Side ducking.

Fast trill—
open grassland,
dense forest.

VI. THE TRIAD OF LIGHT

57

Spire on still lake—
splayed—
midnight green.

Sunk—
flat oval sun—
horizon.

Shimmering hot air
over asphalt—
glistening rainbow oil.

VII. THE TRIAD OF RESOLUTION

65

Cone snap—
eyeshine—
bright litter.

Dew drop
halos—
a blurry blade of grass.

Speckled forest,
light layered on light—
a grainy mouse—smeared.

SECTION III — ECHO

VIII. THE TRIAD OF AFTERFORM

Wet mud on rock—
seeping, drying—
honeycomb face.

White ice—melting.
Black water under sun—
an ocean—swelling.

Skeletons—a cliff wall eroding.
Fossil water—
wild orchid.

IX. THE TRIAD OF TREMBLE

Pedal waves, undulating—
slime trail—
glass.

Flat leaf,
breeze—
quake.

Smeared—
red, orange—
horizon.

X. THE TRIAD OF ECHO

91

Bubbles—
trapped—
a cold spot—hiss.

A duct—
trembling—
whistle—burnt air.

Cool air—
shuddering vent—
cracked coil.

AFTERWORD

Nothing resolves.

Each triad closes only in form. The tension
remains.
That's by design.

This is not a circle.
It's a spiral with one plane collapsed.
A return that doesn't return to the same.

The final fold is not an ending.
It's an echo—
distorted, delayed, but intact.

There is no key.
Only recurrence.
Only trace.

If you feel something unfinished,
you're holding it correctly.

— J. A. Gucci

ACKNOWLEDGMENTS

Thank you to those who understood the work
before I did.

To the friends who didn't ask what it meant.
To the readers who noticed the fold but didn't
flatten it.
To the few who showed up at the right
pressure.

You won't find your names here.
But your presence is in the system.

This book would not have unfolded without
you.
Thank you.

— J. A. Gucci

APPENDIX

THE SYSTEM

Each poem is a triad.
Each triad contains:

- Three stanzas
- Each stanza: three lines
- Each line: one register of pressure

Line 1 — Matter
Concrete, physical, perceptual

Line 2 — Mind
Systems, cognition, movement

Line 3 — Being
State, residue, echo

Each triad belongs to a larger arc:

- **Ground** — contact, resistance, compression
- **Field** — resonance, signal, pattern
- **Echo** — trace, blur, recurrence

There are no metaphors.
Ambiguity is structural.
The reader is responsible for interpretation.

This appendix does not decode.
It confirms the constraints.

ABOUT THE AUTHOR

J. A. Gucci writes in systems, not sentences.
Their work resists metaphor and rewards
compression.

They are the author of Pressure System and the
forthcoming Echo Chamber Music.
The Book of Triads is their second major fold.

They live near water.
They prefer silence to conclusions.

ALSO BY THE AUTHOR

The Twelve Series
> Twelve Small Windows
> Twelve Loops
> Twelve Clay Tablets
> Twelve Desert Floods
> Twelve Marble Questions
> Twelve Roman Thresholds

The Paradox Trilogy
> Diction I: The Paradox of Feeling
> Diction II: The Paradox of Faith
> Diction III: The Paradox of Reflection

Pressure System
Failure Modes

COLOPHON

The Book of Triads was written and structured
by J. A. Gucci.
No metaphors were used.
The system was discovered, not designed.

The manuscript was composed using [insert
software, e.g. Scrivener, InDesign, etc. if you
wish],
and typeset in [insert font(s) used — or omit
for anonymity].

The layout follows a triadic logic:
Three arcs — Ground, Field, Echo.
Each poem contains three stanzas of three lines
each.
Each line corresponds to a perceptual register:
Matter, Mind, Being.

This edition was printed in the United States in
the year 2026.